Random Words of Poetry

(Abstract "Word Art" On Paper)

Email: breezeartanddesign@gmail.com

Breeze ©2019

(All Rights Reserved)

ISBN 978-0-578-44607-3

(Eagle Eye Publishing)

Acknowledgements

For family members, good friends, well-wishers far and near that have supported me throughout the years. Not least, for the many poetry lovers and poetry discoverers everywhere. This book is for you.

About the Author

Born in (what is now called) Kingston, Jamaica. I became a part of the 1948—1972 "Windrush Generation" after migrating to England in 1965 aged eight, where I was reunited with my mother who had become a part of an earlier "Windrush Generation" when she migrated from Jamaica in 1960. I lived in England for over twenty years through grade school, college into adulthood, then migrated to the United States in 1986 and became a citizen. Eventually, I returned to live in England for a few years. Then I lived in Jamaica, where I became more aware of varying aspects of my island home. I now reside in the United States once again. Living in all three countries twice has been the inspiration for some of my writings.

Introduction

Coloring, writing and producing creative art has been a part of my life since childhood. In 1967 then headmaster Mr. Garth, of Crawford Road Primary School in South East London, shut down a lunch time play I had created and directed because too many screams and loud laughter was coming from the art room we used to stage that epic, about ghosts.
My first acclaimed poem was created at the same school between grades three to four. It recounted a hurricane experience whilst living with my grandmother in the hills of Jamaica. It was a holistic feeling, reciting to the receptive audience of my peers and teachers who reciprocated with enthusiastic applause. That poem made the wall of honor. It is possible I could have gone on to study literary art but studied visual art and design instead, while continuing to produce poetry and song lyrics as a hobby. I am happy to be sharing some of my writings with you here, where you will find poetic references from my childhood to more recent and varied themes within this first publication entitled, *Random Words of Poetry (*Abstract Word Art on *Paper.*)
Giving much thanks.

Table of Contents

1. Acknowledgements 3
4. About the Author 3
5. Introduction 3
6. Contents 5
7. I Searched 7
8. Poetry in Motion 8
9. School Friends Five 9
10. Photograph 9
11. Sitting on the Shore of Time 10
12. Poetry Gets Boring 11
13. Life Is a Journey 12
14. Power Up 13
15. Females 14
16. A "Relationship Handler" 15
17. The Mark of The Beast 16
18. Rolled Models 17
19. We Are Use to Saying "Tribes" 18
20. A Thought Filled Moment 19
21. Why Spend Time 19
22. Some Be Ignoring Seniors 20
23. How Many of Us 21
24. Elders Are Roots 21
25. Introduction to Windrushed 22 - 24
26. A Little Rich Girl 25
27. Windrushed 26 - 27
28. In My Country 28 - 29
29. Missing Home 30
30. Fine 30
31. The Departed 31
32. The Further Out We Travelled 32
33. No Thing Wrote 32
34. Sometimes 33
35. Once We Get Tired 33
36. Poem Star 34
37. Works of Art 35
38. Photograph of the Author 37
39. Notes 39 – 40

Upon Pondering

The journeys of Christopher Columbus
I Searched
To find my origins

And Discovered

I came before labels

February 23rd 2018

Poetry in Motion

Water

Like abstract canvas
Throw out gems
From the ocean

To the world

Large swift voluminous
Hues of blues
Greys
Splashing
White
Tiny silver shimmers

From deep fluid waters night

Bright

March 2016

School Friends Five

On a beach front

Waves lapping
Wind blowing
Tiny particles of sand

Young sisters' cousins' relatives' friends' or neighbors'

Ad lib pose

Capturing an abstract moment

Of their fun filled day

January 7th 2017

January 7th 2017

Sitting On the Shore Of Time

Observing each one as they enter
Emerging between closely built fish huts
Onto beachfront shore line

Elders amongst them
Burst into intermittent childlike smiles
Their tongues swipe lips
At the expectancy of sea water on skin

Seagull soaring air touch their faces
Without making direct contact
Whispering secrets of the ocean
In a language they had forgotten
Because they have stayed away for so long
Vital foreboding air telegraphs of the future wisk bye bye

Another group descends on sand
Laughing children scream between lost tooth smiles
With *unshore* of the water voices
Rushing into
Then running away from
Splashing waves they do not know how to swim in

He and her couple arrive to play their love game
Commencing a bizarre water ritual
Boosting ego to where it cannot enter
Without this act that becomes like a fix

Sitting on the shore of time watching
As beachfront transformations occur within peoples

January 26th 2017

Poetry Gets Boring

If it ain't real
Sometimes raw
Captures of things

In fear free different perspective

For ones to like
Dislike
Be offended
Be blissed
Be lost
Found
Discussed

Poetry is boring when tapered to fit into what is not its self

Free flowing be

Until the blinder begin to *sea*

Poetry ain't poetry when censored

To another ones

Taste

April 19th 2018

Life Is a Journey

That can make you shout get one out
Into unexpected situations for better or seemingly worse

While driving do not take your eyes off the road
Read the signs obey laws man made spiritual
Plan your journey as best you can
But know
You might be on a journey of discovery
That is not always plan-able
Travel with your map
Have your gps (real meditations) as guide
Do not pick up strangers' unfamiliar spirits along the way
Keep your vehicle self
Clean and cared for
Exercise as you do
Eat sleep think and rest
Run Tai Chi Yoga maybe into a life
Substance abuse free
Being conscious what type of fuels
One puts into ones system
What elements one may expose themselves to

No negative entities in your place or space
Do they cause yourself to change into negativity too
That you are not
Do they seduce you
Draining vital forces for frivolous gain
Watch the road

Life is a journey   March 13th 2017 – February 2019

Power Up

Do not let that thing into your core
The thing that jumps from person to person
Finding hosts
It infects a susceptible mind
Controlling it in an instant

Persons you think you once knew
Family friend acquaintance become possessed
With a personality that is not theirs to keep
A momentarily borrowed body
Power up
If you can withstand
Their real self may come back tomorrow later today or when
Power up
Do not let that thing in
That attacks
It can push one to anger
Rip precious substances
From ones being

Dressed

In Pradarian fancies or down to earth gear
Wrapped in a bundle of false pretense

It moves slowly

Fast out of control blinding lights heading toward precipices
With its victims
Attached
Power up

February 23rd 2018

Females

Liken unto sponges
Soaking up a deceptive one
While in ecstasy and fantasy
To parents they do not listen
Worse once the damage has been done
The ego hides in fluids
That can hold a heinous mind
Woe unto her
Who bucks upon the wrong
In subtle sin-cer-ity

A sponge like mind captured

To the bidding of the out of control
La femmes
Do be careful
Among whom you choose to roll

Here comes the treasured image
Of his parent's soul
Being swiftly captured
Through enchantments of sweet venom
He falls to her calls
Becoming ensnared
With her puppeteering handlers
Hiding in the wings
Waiting there to reap
Once she lulls him to sleep

To parents they do not listen
Worse once the damage has been done

April 1st 2018

A "Relationship Handler"

Comes into one's life pretentiously disguised
Always there when needed
A dependable friend
Some come freaking rocking worlds asunder
Whilst introducing porn
Who haphazardly brings along lascivious
Now all order gets thrown out of order
From their purest paths
Forlorn stumbling sucked strengths blinded seers
A "Handlers" duties has been performed

Others mate for offspring's to be used
Recruited from the womb

One may begin to think they are in love

With the "Handler"
Who has them hooked lined and sinkered
Mesmerized
But that is their duties call
Toward a greater cause of those who sent them
Methodically infiltrating bloodlines
Yet unawaken to who they really are
Blackmailers
Entwiners well trained and paid
Your owner things including offspring's they try to glean
Thinking they know how to control one's head
Calculating whilst dictating the way one's life should go
Be aware
Of "The Handler Reaper"
Reaping as it sows

April 22nd 2018

The Mark of the Beast

Is my phone
In the palm of my hand
Its microphone
Records all of my noises
Some of its apps collect
My photographs
Whether I want them to or not
While its camera spies
At times
My phone seems
Like a trusted friend
Recording my poetic thoughts
Helping me to remember
What I sometimes forget
Scheduling me accurately
It plays the sounds I want to hear
Lulling me to sleep
Entertaining me with moving pictures
That once
Could only be found
On a big screen
My phone is cleverer than I
When doing math
But I am betterer than it
When doing art
It might be radiating me
I won't find out
Until I say when
Do not touch my phone
It is a beast
And a sort
Of good friend

January 21st 2017

Rolled Models

Are manufactured beings clothed as free people
Set in places
Fooling masses to agendas
Whilst touting one another
They all sound the repetitive boring same

Inspirators

Original beings
Show light to people
Whilst maneuvering in free spaces
Content with adoration admirations
You are not here to follow see
They allow real peoples
Themselves to be

January 22nd 2017 – May 2018

We Are Used to Saying "Tribes"

Pertaining to a group from a particular race location
Outside the box there are specific "tribes"
Scattered within many nations

There could be a blood related family
Of say five people
Each one of a different "tribe"
Dishes in the sink "tribe"
Spotlessly clean "tribe"

So do not stress
If you do not understand
A family member friend or co-worker

They come from a different "tribe" to you

July 5th 2016 - March 22nd 2018

A Thought Filled Moment

Out of a sunny day
Here where we stay

For our true love in life
My lens reverence nature
While expressing myself to you
In precious moments of busy times
Hither dear
See how
This interpreted scene
Holds abstract greens
Lights
Chaotically mathematically spiritually sensually encasing
Bloomed speaking petals
Anther filament embodiment completes
A truly captured aspect
Of my dearest love for you

February 8th 2017

Why Spend Time

Wishing for years
That have floated on
Why spend time
Wishing for years
That will arrive
When they come
Why not explore
And embrace
The corridors
Of our currents

February 23rd 2018

Some be ignoring seniors

Although some seniors hold life
In the palm of their conscious hands
There are those who be disrespecting seniors
Unless they have dollar values
For sum to snake

There are those seniors who carry resentful feelings
Toward their juniors for things
Juniors know not about
With bitterness of heart from the past
For days years lifetimes go on these things
Spreading hurtful infections
Through multiple generations
Sometimes even to their greats

They show no change

Some seniors
Do abuse their juniors
With the kind forgiving hearts

We should know by now
How
These things once had a start

When will these cycles end

March 31st 2018

How Many Of Us

Can protect the child within
When worlds around us
Try to force its abandonment

March 2016 – March 20th 2018

Elders Are Roots

Children seeds
We be trunks
Branches
Fruits
Leaves

Care for the roots
Care for the seeds
Care for the whole being

Tree of life

June 6th 2016

Introduction to Windrushed

When I speak some folks say
Where is your accent from
Africa Australia New Zealand
When I say England they ask
How did you get over there
Pain
Emotions begin to swell

Individual stories are like many big ships
Small boats on huge oceans
Some speed some sail some sink
Never to be told
This poem speaks of HMS Windrush (aka Empire)
That nearly sunk
A particular family
From a particular tribe of people
Originating within a tricked transplanted generation
From a country now called Jamaica

Many were lured away from their Island homes
By invitation to a place they were taught to call
"The Mother Country"
They were asked to help rebuild
What was left of Hitler's hate
After the second world war of our times
Wave after wave they arrived
1940's 50's 60's 70's to cold Britain
Not expecting to see signs on homes for rent
Reading no dogs no wogs (aka negros)
No Irish
Not expecting for so many new faces to ask a little girl
What brought you from sunshine to this cold place

Not expecting elderly females to rub your hands
And arms for good luck
As if they knew something about you that you did not

Instead

Transplanted "Indians" west of those times
Expected to help rebuild
As they were invited to
Earn and return
To their own beautiful island homes in sunshine
There had been no vision of becoming stuck
For generations of broken families
Broken homes
Broken expectations

Meanwhile back home in what is now called Jamaica
Uninvited rats and mice play
In abodes belonging to trusting cats
Who have been wronged for what is rightfully theirs
Not any who feels it knows it voices
Have risen
From returning residents
Of particular families
From particular tribe nations
Of those deceived transplanted generations
Who
Upon returning home after many years in the cold
Are repeatedly robbed killed or hounded
Out of their own country
Back into cold
While smiling faces greet unsuspecting vacationers
As if ongoing ethnic cleansing has not been taking place

Over the past many years 1940's 50's 60's 70's now

Cloned out communities

Something's not right
A tiny island
With one of the highest murder rates
In a big world
Research of past and present island news
Show daily doses
Of lewd tactics
Replacement faces
Fake histories
Being used
To further try and destroy (ethnically cleanse)
These particular aboriginal tribes

April 30th – August 15th 2018

A Little Rich Girl

Protected by mountains at aged three

When mother became Windrushed
I had my house on my land with goats and clean air
In my own country
Drinking fresh milk for breakfast and Cerasee for tea
I bathed in cool clear spring waters
Glistening sun kissed coconut oiled skin
Carefully dressed in prettily sewn frocks
Accessorized with precious metal bangles
To step with family
Into ceremonial occasions
Some Saturdays mostly Sundays though

Early rising 4am Linstead market outing observations
Showed me simple folks feed nations
As I drank jelly coconut water from its source
While resting closely to my Grannie
Good people called me her "Handbag"
All that love belonged to me

Sheets of ice floating holding
Funny looking houses on the top
Was a seven year olds 1960's imaginings
About a place she did not know
A place suddenly thrusted into
With a white thing
Called snow

A still connected more protected Rich Girl
I have not lost me   November 1965 - April 2019

Windrushed

Hush
You will see your mother again soon
She soon send for you to go to England
Until that time come
Your Grannie going to look after you now

Three years passed

Grannie cannot manage country life and you
She will come to visit in Kingston every month
You going to town to live with your Gran Auntie B

But no one told this child about the witch tenant
Her two daughters and one's three year old baby girl
Spreading tales telling lies
Making sure
She caught a beating every weekend
How much can a five year old take
(Straight up ones do not trust some types who now call themselves what is now called Jamaican)

Nearly three more years later

Hush be happy you going to England now
Let us burn your hair
Ouch
Stop di crying nuh
Oh you have been speaking good English
Now it's time to speak even better..
Windrushed prepped
Onto a B.O.A.C. plane
(British Overseas Airways Corporation)

Dressed in fall clothing for a winter storm
Lawd look pon the thin gloves them send her in
Unto cold flight
Not even a coat
What they do with the money I send them
Mother is a stranger
Grannie is alone
But I did leave her my shiny new transistor radio
For company
I wonder if she can hear me through it from here
Is St. Mary really that far from London

Dear Grannie
I got the air letter you sent me from Flint River PO
In the hills of Jamaica
Sorry to hear the price of
Rice gaan up
Sugar gaan up
Flour gaan up
I will help you when I get big
Yes I am trying hard in school
Although it is very cold
Grannie my talk is changing to thingy-mi-jig

Windrushed
Hushed

This is a part of where I came from

That is how I got over there

April 30th 2018

In My Country

(Now known as Jamaica)
There are many mansions there
Big new unfinished homes
Among many more empty ones
Next to more half built ones
Down the lane
Sitting beside captured yards and lands

Occupied
By unrelated relations
Because their true owners have been away
Far too long

You see that one next door
Turning grey black and green
While waiting too long to be completed
Lived in
Filled with love and family celebrations
Many more are like that
Empty
Lonely
Longing for their family's return

They who are
Windrushed aboriginal peoples
They whose aboriginal descendants
Got stuck
In British council things
Called council houses or council flats
Or aboriginal reservations

What a trade-off
For a yard with mango trees
Cool breeze warm shores
With once abundantly filled seas
Aboriginal peoples
Stuck in British hospitals
Pounding cold roads
Over spilling filling
Mental institutions
Jails
Graves
Empty and lonely
Yearning for their once peaceful homes

Some still do not realize they are being robbed
Of their legacies
By seemingly smooth criminals
(Some of whom seemingly look similar to our own selves)
Never having a chance to return to one's own island home
No vacations
Too many of those who do make it back there
Die
Too soon after their arrival
Or
They have to pack up and leave again
Running for their lives

Grass grows tall
Over unfinished homes
While legacies are stolen
Windrushed hushed
No more

October 15th 2018

Missing Home

On a cold day

In transit anywhere
USA Canada UK

Memory glimpses
Of a sea bath
At the beginning of a hot day

During the ride from
A 9 to 5

February 26th 2018

Fine

They say they are fine
Whilst hurting badly
Mental health
Affects us all
Sadly

June 2018

The Departed

Search air
Looking
For compassionate souls
To complain to
About their demise
Telling stories
Of what transpired

When
How
Whom

The departed have voices
To connect
That are current
Long after they are gone

March 13th 2017

The Further Out We Travelled

The more our innocence
Got taken away
To that hard to reclaim place
Now stored
Somewhere deep inside
Of one's own
Unconscious space

May 6th 2018

No Thing Wrote

Last night
To change this light
No morning after pill
To take

For verse

March 26th 2018

Sometimes

An Experience
Is
A way to find
Out
Not stay in

2016

Once We Get Tired

Of being fooled
We set out
To be found

2017

I'm a Poem Star Baby

I know my life has gold diamonds platinum
Jeweled filled meanings
Ever living shiny great
No matter how ones try to bring down and beret
I'm a poem star baby
Earned through eons
Years of being uniquely me
Signed sealed delivered
A gem born through times of struggles to be free
A visual artist with the ability to bring spirit to the fore
A designer of abstract conscious patterns placed
Many types more
A lyricist creating melodies who can sing
I set gems
Don't you dare tell me I am worth no thing
I'm a poem star baby
Thee keeper of treasure troves since creation of the core
With all these energetic gifts I know I have vibes to pour
All four corners connected earth water-way fire wind
Are integral parts of me knowing
What I need to know about things
Please
Do not categorize me into abcz
Expecting me to stay where I do not belong
Kicking down doors my peoples sisters brothers
Are not whores
Possessing keys that can never be permanently taken
Rearranged or changed
A poem star baby
Naturally gifted
All the way

April 25th 2018 - February 17th 2019

I See People as Works of Art

Accepting individuals for whom they portray
Or what they really are from start
Working on what needs to be within myself
Whilst knowing well many out there
Will remain what they star

I see people's purple hearts
Their glittery sparks
Beautifully covered gemstone selves
Their little tiny elves
Humongous hideous hidden behaviors

I see people as works of art

Abstractly sprung from corrugated conflicts
Confusion of minds
Lack of knowledge don't *sea* self
As priceless originals needing protection
Conservation not to be rearranged

So what if ones are outside so-called normal *reign*
Plop-o-ti-plot tiny dots
More than a spot
You decorate a universal gallery

I see people as works of art

September 17th 2018 – February 19th 2019

Author & Artist Breeze

NOTES

www.ingramcontent.com/pod-product-compliance
Lightning Source LLC
Chambersburg PA
CBHW041308110426
42743CB00037B/36